Contents

Skilful hands

Sleight of hand is one of the most important skills a magician can learn. It means to move something with your hands without letting anyone see what you are doing. Good magicians use sleight of hand all the time – hiding coins behind their fingers and tucking cards up their sleeves.

(1) Preparation

Sometimes you may need to prepare part of the trick before you start your performance.

Putting on a show

Magic is as much about the performance as it is about the tricks. This is very true of sleight-of-hand tricks where it is important that your audience does not notice what is really going on. The more you can entertain your audience, by telling jokes and stories, the easier it will be for you to distract them from the secrets of the tricks.

(2) Difficulty rating

The tricks get harder throughout the book, so each trick has been given a rating. One is the easiest and seven is the hardest. The most difficult tricks will take a bit of practice to get right, but the results will be worth it!

Hidden hanky

Having shown your audience that the is nothing in your hands and nothin your sleeves, you rub your hands toget the magic words, 'hey presto', and sudd handkerchief has appeared.

(1)

Preparation

• Fold up the handkerchief as small as it will go.

• Now push the arms of your top up very slightly, just a couple of centimetres, so that folds begin to appear in the elbow join. Now hide the rolled-up handkerchief in one of the folds.

Props needed...

The props you will need throughout the book.

- Books
- Chair
- Coins
- Deck of cards
- Dice
- Elastic band
- Envelope
- Grape
- Handkerchief

- Ice cubes
- Jacket or top with long sleeves
- Jug of water
- Paper
- Pen
- Pencil
- Plastic tumbler
- Round-bodied glass

- Ruler
- Scissors
- Sponge
- Sponge ball
- Sticky tape
- Table
- White plastic cup

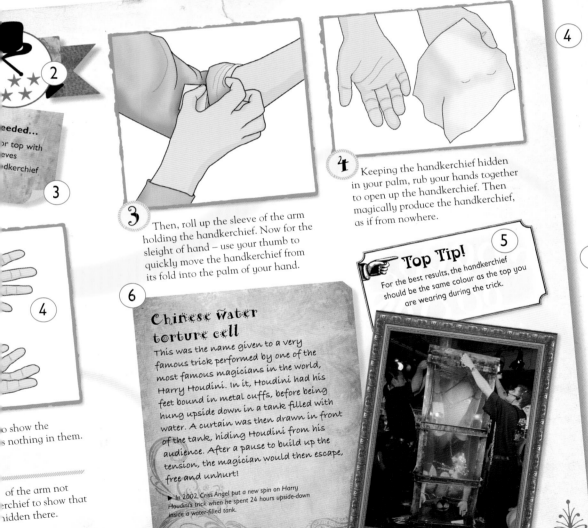

③ Then, roll up the sleeve of the arm holding the handkerchief. Now for the sleight of hand – use your thumb to quickly move the handkerchief from its fold into the palm of your hand.

④ Keeping the handkerchief hidden in your palm, rub your hands together to open up the handkerchief. Then magically produce the handkerchief, as if from nowhere.

⑤ **Top Tip!**
For the best results, the handkerchief should be the same colour as the top you are wearing during the trick.

Chinese water torture cell

This was the name given to a very famous trick performed by one of the most famous magicians in the world, Harry Houdini. In it, Houdini had his feet bound in metal cuffs, before being hung upside down in a tank filled with water. A curtain was then drawn in front of the tank, hiding Houdini from his audience. After a pause to build up the tension, the magician would then escape, free and unhurt!

► In 2002, Criss Angel put a new spin on Harry Houdini's trick when he spent 24 hours upside-down inside a water-filled tank.

④ **Stages and illustrations**

Step-by-step instructions, as well as illustrations, will guide you through each trick.

⑤ **Top Tip!**

Hints and tips help you to perform the tricks better!

⑥ **Famous magicians and illusions**

Find out who are the most exciting and skilful magicians, and what amazing feats they have performed.

The Wobbly pencil

This trick is a simple optical illusion. The secret is learning how to move the pencil at just the right speed to make it look rubbery. Practise this before performing the trick in front of an audience.

1

Ask a volunteer from the audience to inspect the pencil to make sure there is nothing unusual about it.

2

Tell your volunteer that you are going to turn the pencil into rubber. Wave your hands over the pencil as if you are performing a magic spell, and say the magic word, 'abracadabra'.

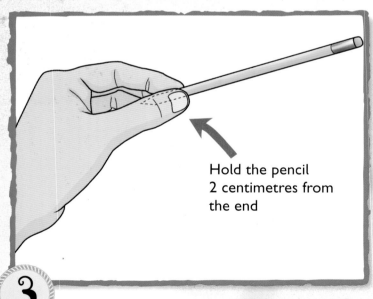

Hold the pencil 2 centimetres from the end

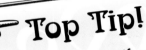

Top Tip!

The more you act as if you have 'magic powers', the more your audience will believe you.

3

Now, using your thumb and first finger, pick up the pencil about 2 centimetres from the pointed end and hold it horizontally.

gic

DBOOK

HT OF
ND

JOE FULLMAN

Publishing

A catalogue record for this book is available from the British Library.

ISBN 978 1 84835 094 6

Printed and bound in China

Author Joe Fullman
Editor Amanda Askew
Designer Jackie Palmer
Illustrator Mark Turner for Beehive Illustrations

Publisher Steve Evans
Creative Director Zeta Davies

Picture credits
Alamy Mary Evans Picture Library 15
Corbis Reuters 7, Bettmann 11
Getty Images Ethan Miller 19, Matthew Peyton 25, Frederick M Brown 29, 31

4 Holding the pencil lightly in front of you, start to wiggle it up and down. The pencil will appear to go wobbly.

5 After a while, stop wiggling the pencil and wave your free hand over it to make it solid again. Hand the pencil back to your friend, so they can see it is, once again, just an ordinary pencil.

Breaking free

Escapology is a type of magic in which a magician breaks free from something holding them. This can be anything from ropes or handcuffs to chains and straitjackets. Escapologists often rely on sleight of hand to perform their tricks – hiding keys or tools in their hands to help them to escape.

▶ An escapologist from Georgia, Zurab Vadachkoria is handcuffed and locked inside a water-filled tank. He escapes unscathed four minutes later.

instant ice

Y ou pick up the plastic cup, pour in some water, turn it over and, 'hey presto', a couple of ice cubes come tumbling out. The magic for this simple trick is all in the preparation. The clever bit is making sure your audience cannot see what you are really doing.

Props needed...
* Ice cubes
* Jug of water
* Scissors
* Small piece of sponge
* White plastic cup

Preparation

• Cut a small piece of sponge, just slightly bigger than the base of your cup.

• Make sure the sponge is squashed tightly inside the cup and will not fall out when you turn over the cup.

• Now put a couple of ice cubes on top of the sponge.

1 Show the plastic cup to the audience and tell them that you are going to make instant ice cubes.

Top Tip!

When you show the cup, tilt it a little towards the audience, but make sure you do not tip it too far, otherwise they will see the ice cubes.

2 Pick up the jug and pour a couple of centimetres of water into the cup. Unseen by the audience, the sponge will soak up the water.

3 Wave your hand over the cup, say the magic word, 'abracadabra', and turn over the cup, tipping out the ice cubes. To the audience, it will look like the water has instantly frozen.

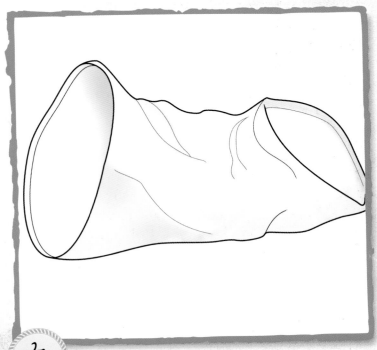

4 Finish the trick by crumpling the cup and throwing it away. This will stop the audience from examining it and working out how the trick is done.

9

The grape olympics

You will need to be very careful when performing this trick, as you will be handling a glass. Make sure there is an adult present before you begin the grape olympics!

Preparation

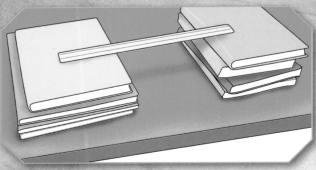

• On a tabletop, use the books and ruler to make a jump.

• Place your grape on one side of the jump, and your glass on top of the grape.

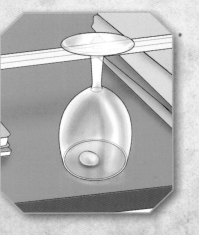

1 Bet your friend that they cannot get the grape to travel over the jump without tipping over the glass or touching the grape with their hands. When they give up, show them how it is done.

Top Tip!

This is a very good trick for improving your 'hand–eye coordination' – an important part of learning how to do sleight-of-hand tricks.

2 Grip the glass and start spinning it around very quickly in small circles. This will create something known as 'centrifugal force', which will make the grape spin around inside the glass.

3 Keep on spinning and lift the glass up and over the jump – without the grape falling out – and put it down on the other side.

Little and large

Some magicians perform small tricks using cards or coins. Others work on a much bigger scale. Harry Blackstone was a US magician who specialized in large illusions, including 'sawing a woman in half' and 'levitation'. Blackstone's most famous trick, however, used a simple light bulb that he would magically make glow and float over the heads of his audience.

▶ Harry Blackstone performs an illusion in which he appears to pull his assistant's head up through a tube.

Two into one

Amaze your audience as you turn two small paper rings into one giant ring. This trick requires important preparation.

Props needed...
* Large piece of paper
* Pencil
* Ruler
* Scissors
* Sticky tape

Preparation

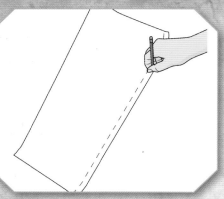

• Take your piece of paper, draw a long rectangle about one metre long by 4 centimetres wide. Cut out the rectangle.

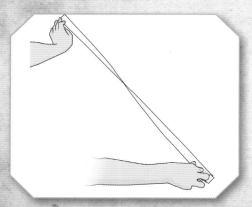

• Attach a piece of sticky tape to one end. Twist the paper once and then stick the ends together.

1

Show your audience the paper ring. Tell them that you are going to cut the ring in half to make two rings.

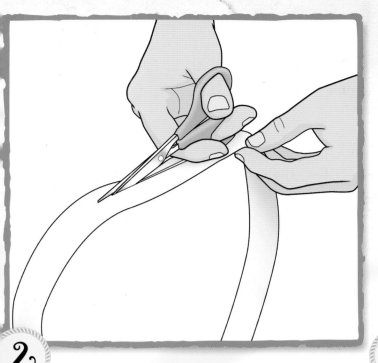

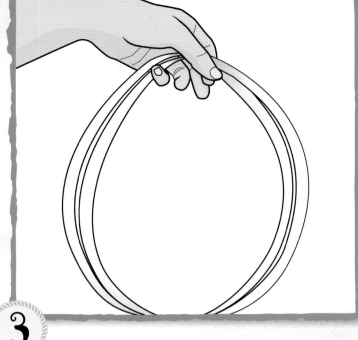

2 Cut the ring lengthways along its middle. As long as you remember to put a twist in the ring, you will not cut it in half. It will just look as if you have.

3 When you have finished, hold the paper in one hand to show that it is now two rings.

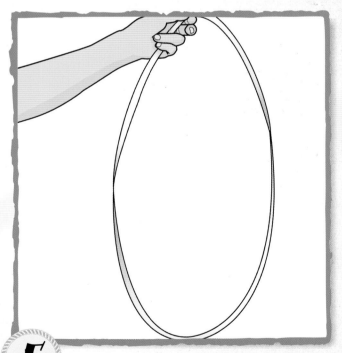

4 Tell your audience that you are now going to magically turn the two small rings into one giant ring. Wave your free hand over the rings, and say the magic word, 'abracadabra'.

5 Now drop the first ring off the front of your fingers, the two rings will now have transformed into one large ring.

Linking rings

This trick is mind boggling. As long as you remember to put two twists in the ring, it should work every time.

Props needed...
* Large piece of paper
* Pencil
* Ruler
* Scissors
* Sticky tape

Preparation

• Make a paper ring out of a long strip of paper, about one metre long by 4 centimetres wide.

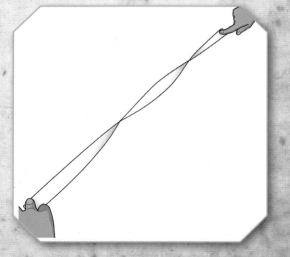

• Before you stick the ends together, twist the strip of paper twice.

1

Show your audience the paper ring. Tell them that you are going to cut the ring to make two separate rings.

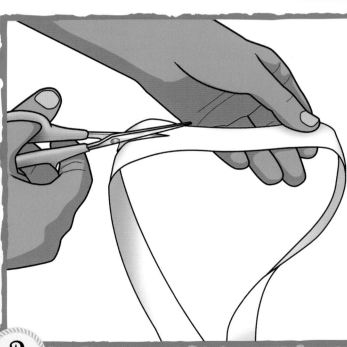

2

Cut the ring lengthways along its middle.

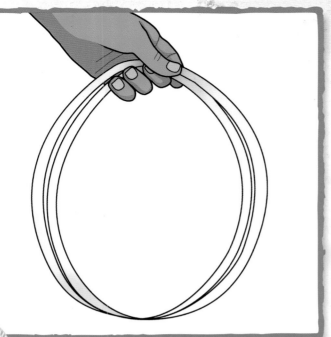

3 Once you have finished, hold the paper in one hand to show that it is now two separate rings.

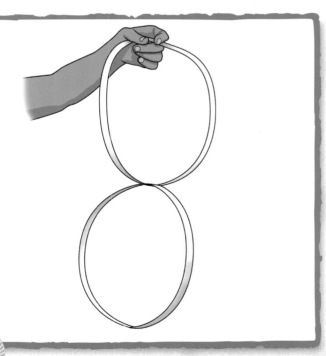

5 Now drop the first ring off the front of your fingers, while keeping hold of the other ring. The two rings will be linked together. It's magic!

4 Tell your audience that you are going to link the rings together. Wave your free hand over the rings, and say the magic word, 'abracadabra'.

▲ *An actor stands dressed as a ghost off-stage where an assistant projects their image onto the stage using John Pepper's special effect. The actor attempts to stab the ghost with his sword but — to the audience's amazement — finds only thin air.*

Pepper's ghost

Some tricks are so good, they are reused by many magicians. In the 19th century, John Pepper invented a stage illusion that used mirrors and special lighting to make objects magically appear and disappear. Today, this same illusion is used at Haunted House attractions in Disney theme parks around the world to make it look as if ghosts are appearing before the audience's eyes.

The magic envelope

T his great mind-reading trick is guaranteed to baffle your audience. You will need to practise the sleight of hand a few times to make sure you always pick up the card and the envelope together. If you get it wrong, your audience will see how the trick is done.

Preparation

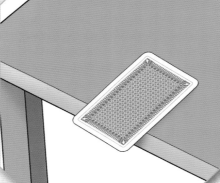

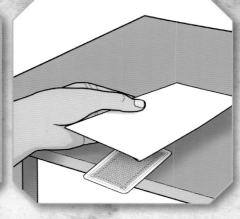

• Remove one of the cards from the deck. It does not matter which one. Write the name of the card on the piece of paper. Seal the paper inside the envelope.

• Place the card face down on the edge of the table with about 2 centimetres of it sticking out over the edge.

• Lay the envelope over the card, so the card is completely covered and part of the envelope is sticking out over the edge of the table, too.

1 Ask a volunteer to shuffle the deck of cards. Tell them that they are going to pick a card and that you have predicted which one they will choose. This is written and sealed inside the envelope.

Top Tip!

It is very important that for step 2, your volunteer does not deal the cards into a neat pile.

2 Once they have thoroughly shuffled the cards, ask your volunteer to start dealing the cards face down onto the table into a rough pile. They can stop whenever they like.

3 When they stop dealing, pick up the envelope and the card beneath it and toss them on top of the pile. It is important to do this quickly and casually, so the audience does not notice the card.

4 Ask your volunteer to open the envelope and read out your prediction.

5 Now turn over the top card, revealing that your prediction was correct!

Jumping elastic

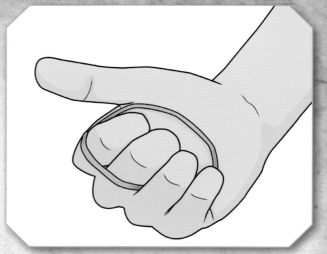

With a simple wave of your hand, an elastic band appears to jump through the air. It is important that you prepare the elastic band in the right way, and master the sleight of hand needed to change its position.

Preparation

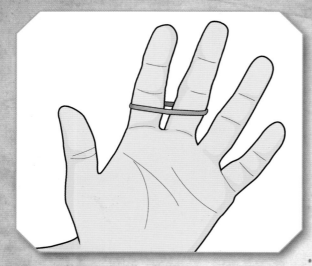

• Stretch out the fingers of your hand and wrap the elastic band around the first two fingers, below the knuckles.

• Curl your fingers into your palm and wrap the band around all four fingers, near your fingernails.

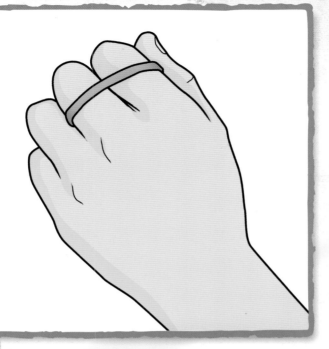

1 Show your audience the back of your hand closed in a fist. Tell them that this is a magic elastic band that can jump through the air.

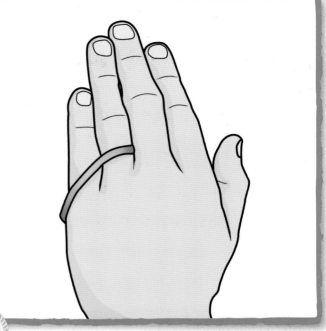

2 Wave your other hand over the band, say the magic word, 'abracadabra', and quickly open out all four fingers of the hand holding the band. The way you have set up elastic band will make it jump onto the other two fingers, as if by magic.

Penn and Teller

Magicians never give away their secrets, unless they are Penn and Teller that is. These two US magicians have a very successful act in which they perform 'impossible illusions', such as being run over by a truck. Then they reveal to their audience exactly how each trick is done.

▶ Penn and Teller's act often features dangerous-looking illusions, which should never be attempted by members of the audience.

Changing spots

This trick shows that you don't need lots of big props to amaze your audience. Sometimes smaller is better. The more smoothly you can perform the sleight of hand, the more magical the trick will seem.

Props needed...
* Small dice

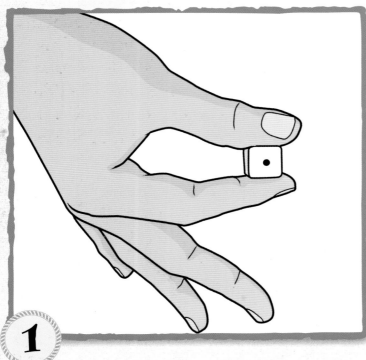

1 Pick up the dice and explain to your audience that this is a magic dice with changing spots. Hold the dice between your finger and thumb and show your audience the number on the front of the dice.

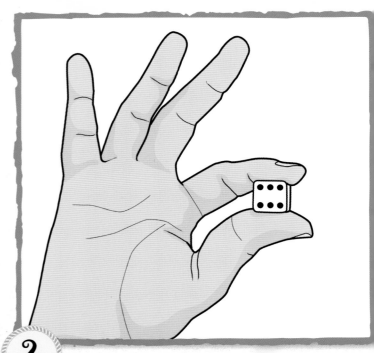

2 Turn your hand over and show the audience the number on the back of the dice.

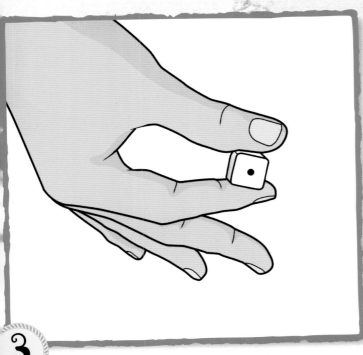

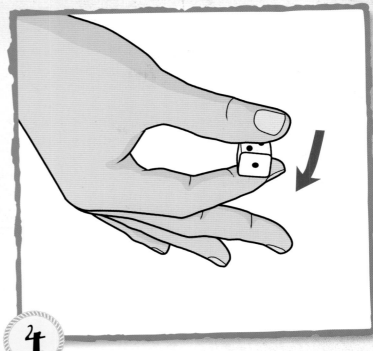

3 Turn your hand back over and show the number on the front of the dice again.

4 Wave your other hand over the dice, and say the magic word, 'abracadabra'. Turn over your hand, as before. This time, as you turn, use your finger and thumb to turn over the dice once. The big movement of your hand will disguise the smaller movement of your fingers.

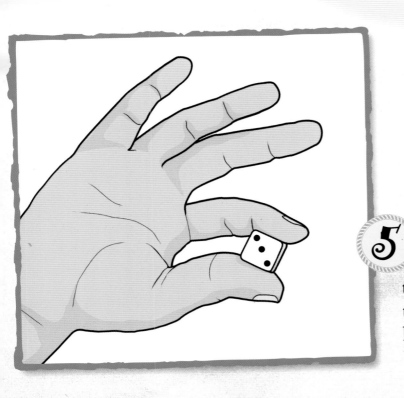

Top Tip!

Waving your other hand over the hand that is holding the dice will distract the audience, and stop them from focusing on what you are doing.

5 Show the audience the number on the back of the dice – with your hand in the same position as step 2. The number has magically changed.

The vanishing cup

This trick uses two special skills – sleight of hand and misdirection. The audience will be concentrating so hard on the coin that they won't notice what you are actually doing.

Props needed...
* Chair
* Paper
* Plastic tumbler
* Table

Preparation

To perform this trick you need to be seated at a table with your legs tucked underneath.

1   Place the coin on the table and put the tumbler over the coin. Tell the audience that you are going to make the coin disappear.

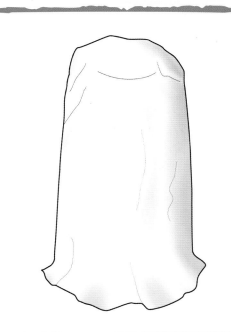

2   Now wrap a piece of paper tightly around the tumbler so that you can see the shape of the tumbler underneath.

3 Lift up the tumbler and the paper to show the audience that the coin is still there. While they are looking at the coin, move the paper towards you to the edge of the table. Then drop the tumbler out of the paper into your lap. The paper should keep the shape of the tumbler, making it look as if it is still there.

4 Now put the tumbler-shaped paper back over the coin. Your audience will believe that it still contains the tumbler.

Top Tip!

You need to perform this sleight of hand carefully, so as not to arouse your audience's suspicions. Hopefully, the audience will be looking at the coin and won't really notice what you are doing.

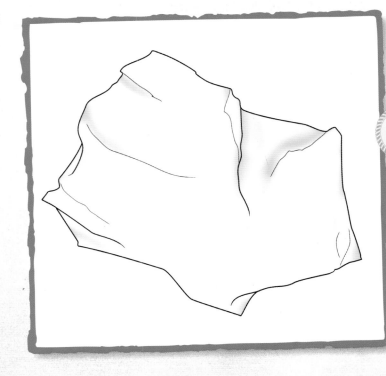

5 Say the magic word, 'abracadabra', and then suddenly smash down your hand on the paper, showing that the tumbler has vanished. Say something like "Oops, that's the problem with magic. Looks like I made the wrong thing disappear." Little do they know, you've made the right thing disappear!

Hidden hanky

Having shown your audience that there is nothing in your hands and nothing up your sleeves, you rub your hands together, say the magic words, 'hey presto', and suddenly a handkerchief has appeared.

Props needed...
* Jacket or top with long sleeves
* Thin handkerchief

Preparation

• Fold up the handkerchief as small as it will go.

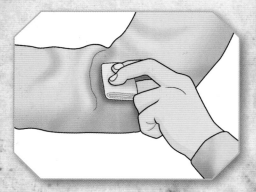

• Now push the arms of your top up very slightly, just a couple of centimetres, so that folds begin to appear in the elbow join. Now hide the rolled-up handkerchief in one of the folds.

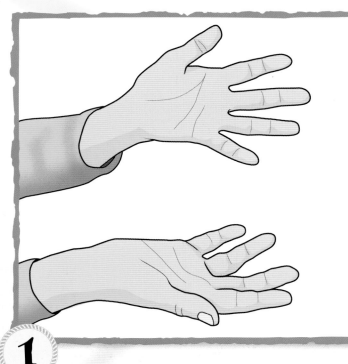

1 Open your hands to show the audience that there is nothing in them.

2 Roll up the sleeve of the arm not holding the handkerchief to show that you have nothing hidden there.

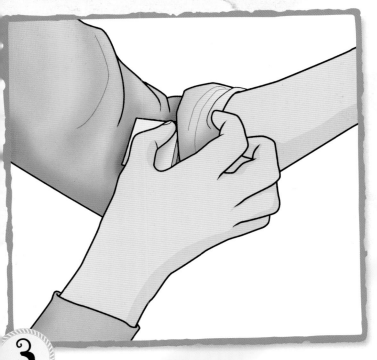

3 Then, roll up the sleeve of the arm holding the handkerchief. Now for the sleight of hand – use your thumb to quickly move the handkerchief from its fold into the palm of your hand.

4 Keeping the handkerchief hidden in your palm, rub your hands together to open up the handkerchief. Then magically produce the handkerchief, as if from nowhere.

Top Tip!

For the best results, the handkerchief should be the same colour as the top you are wearing during the trick.

Chinese Water torture cell

This was the name given to a very famous trick performed by one of the most famous magicians in the world, Harry Houdini. In it, Houdini had his feet bound in metal cuffs, before being hung upside down in a tank filled with water. A curtain was then drawn in front of the tank, hiding Houdini from his audience. After a pause to build up the tension, the magician would then escape, free and unhurt!

▶ In 2002, Criss Angel put a new spin on Harry Houdini's trick when he spent 24 hours upside-down inside a water-filled tank.

Going, going, gone

You show your audience a coin and announce that you are going to make it melt through the table. You place the coin flat on the table, and start rubbing its top with your finger. Amazingly, the coin starts to disappear!

1

Sit at the table with your legs tucked well underneath.

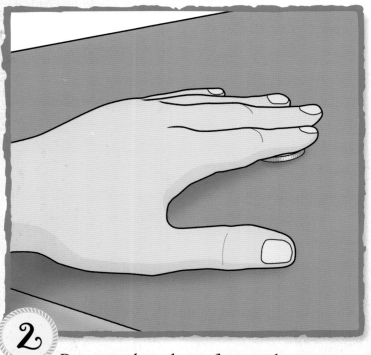

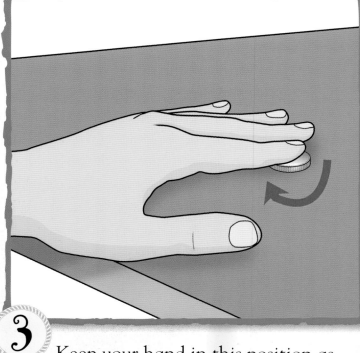

2

Put your hand out flat, with your wrist on the edge of the table. Extend all four fingers and keep them held tightly together. Place the coin on the table, under your first finger.

3

Keep your hand in this position as you begin to rub the top of the coin, using small circular movements.

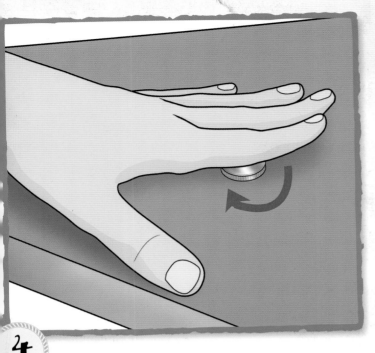

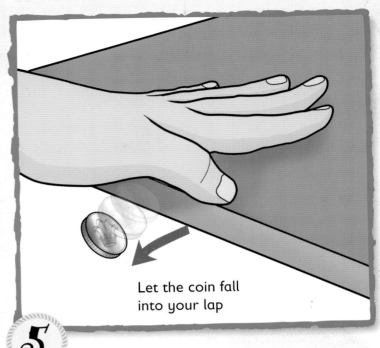

Let the coin fall
into your lap

4 After a few rubs, start moving the coin backwards under your hand, out of sight of the audience.

5 Keep rubbing your finger on the table, as if the coin were still there, all the time using the motion of your hand to move the coin backwards. Once it gets to the back of your hand, allow the coin to slip off the table into your lap.

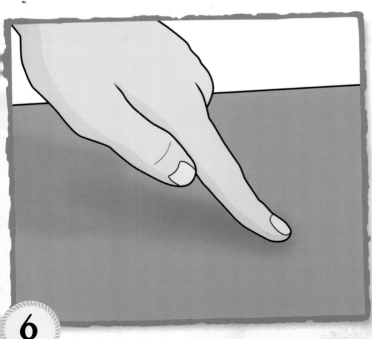

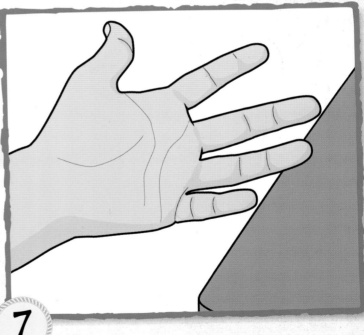

6 Once the coin is in your lap, raise your hand in the air and press the tip of your first finger onto the table. Make a final few rubs, so it looks like you are getting rid of the last of the coin.

7 Lift your hand to show that the coin has completely disappeared. Magic!

The hand pass

This trick is all about speed and accuracy, and will take practice to get right. The result, however, is guaranteed to puzzle your audience.

Props needed...
* Coin

1 Place the coin into the palm of your hand, near the thumb.

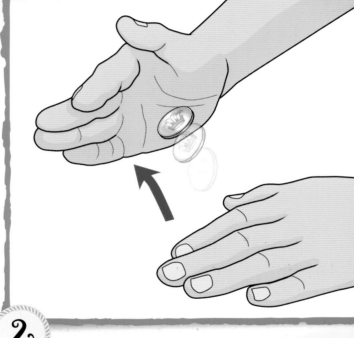

2 This is the tricky bit. Quickly turn over both hands. You are going to flick the coin from one hand under the other. Make sure you turn the hand catching the coin just after the hand flipping the coin, so that there is room for it to go under.

Top Tip!

It is best to perform this trick on a soft surface, so that the coin will not make a noise when it lands.

3 Ask a volunteer to say which hand the coin is under. They obviously pick the hand they last saw the coin in.

4 They are, of course, wrong. You turn over your hands over to reveal that the coin has magically switched hands.

Misdirecting the audience

Whether big or small, all tricks rely on the audience not noticing what is really going on. One way of fooling the audience is to use sleight of hand. Another is to employ a technique called misdirection. This means doing lots of things that have nothing to do with the trick, such as telling jokes or waving a wand. This distracts the audience's attention and directs them away from the secrets of the magic.

◀ *Lance Burton performs the famous 'sawing a woman in half' trick live on US television. Of course, the woman is not really harmed. The magician uses his skills to stop the audience from working out what is really happening.*

Hole in the head

This is all about smoothness and timing. To fool your audience, you will have to get the performance of this piece of sleight of hand just right.

Props needed...
* Small sponge ball

1 Pick up a sponge ball and place it in the centre of your hand.

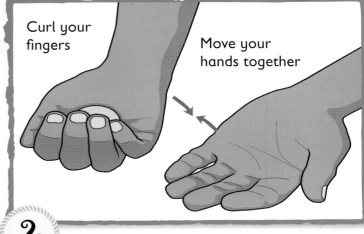

Curl your fingers

Move your hands together

2 Keeping both hands palm up, start moving your hands together. As you do, start curling the fingers of the hand holding the ball towards you.

3 When your hands are close together, move the hand not holding the ball in front of the other hand. This will hide the ball from the audience.

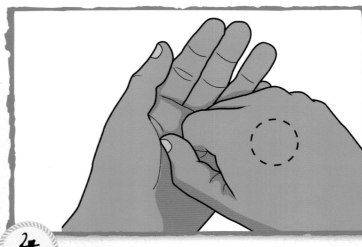

4 Now turn over the hand holding the ball.

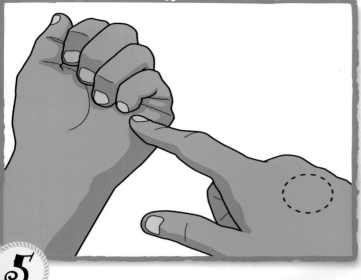

5 As you turn your hand, curl three of your fingers around the ball. At the same time, curl all of the fingers of your other hand towards your palm as if you have just taken hold of the ball.

6 With your empty hand, which the audience believes is now holding the ball, tap yourself lightly on the head.

7 As you tap yourself, raise the hand that is actually holding the ball up to your mouth.

8 Put your hand over your mouth and pretend to cough. Bring your hand away, showing that it now contains the ball. It will look like the ball has travelled right through your head!

Birds from thin air

Channing Pollock was a US magician who could perform many clever tricks using cards and handkerchiefs. However, he became famous above all for one particular illusion – his ability to produce live doves 'from the air'. Pollock eventually left his career as a magician to become an actor in Hollywood.

▶ *Channing Pollock displays his amazing sleight of hand with a pack of cards. He was one of the most skilful magicians of his day.*

The seven principles

The magicians Penn and Teller are well known for explaining the secrets behind their tricks.

According to them, all sleight-of-hand tricks rely on the same skills, which they call the 'seven principles of sleight of hand'. They have one particular illusion that they use to demonstrate these skills. In the trick, Teller appears to repeatedly get rid of a small object and then get a new one. However, it is then revealed that he is actually using the same object the whole time! Penn explains the principles while Teller performs.

▲ *Penn (centre) and Teller (left) receive an award to celebrate performing their magic show in Las Vegas, USA, for five years.*

The seven principles are…

Ditch
To secretly remove an object that is no longer needed.

Load
To secretly move an object to where it is needed.

Misdirection
To direct attention away from what you are actually doing.

Palm
To hold an object in a hand that seems empty.

Simulation
To make it appear that something has happened when it actually hasn't.

Steal
To secretly get an object that is needed.

Switch
To secretly swap one object for another.